The Procrastinator's Perpetual Planner

RED-LETTER PRESS, INC.
SADDLE RIVER, NEW JERSEY

THE PROCRASTINATOR'S PERPETUAL PLANNER
Copyright © 1988 Red-Letter Press, Inc.
ISBN: 0-940462-09-5
Printed in the United States of America
For information address Red-Letter Press, Inc.,
P.O. Box 393, Saddle River, N.J. 07458

INTRODUCTION

Coming soon.

Jack Kreismer
Publisher

ACKNOWLEDGEMENT

Belated thanks to the following procrastinators for their dilatory efforts in contributing to this delayed edition of *The Procrastinator's Perpetual Planner:*

Leona Balcezak
Cyndi Bellerose
Russ Edwards
Glenn Fraller
Sylvia Martin
Jack Kreismer Sr.
Geoff Scowcroft

Special mention is accorded to the founder and president of the Procrastinators' Club of America, truly a man whose time has never come, Les Waas.

THE PROCRASTINATOR'S PRAYER

*Now I lay me down to sleep,
I pray to God, my soul to keep,
Though you'll take it sooner
or later,
I hope, like me, you're a
procrastinator.*

PERSONAL INFORMATION

The Late _____
                    (name)

Lately of _____
                 (address)

_____ Zip _____
       (city/state)

Telephone _____

Resolutions I never got around to last year and probably won't get around to this year:

_____

_____

_____

_____

_____

_____

_____

_____

_____

_____

_____

_____

_____

_____

_____

_____

This is the year you expected so much from last year.

—*Ed Howe*

1989	1990	1991
JANUARY	JANUARY	JANUARY
S M T W T F S	S M T W T F S	S M T W T F S
1 2 3 4 5 6 7	1 2 3 4 5 6	1 2 3 4 5
8 9 10 11 12 13 14	7 8 9 10 11 12 13	6 7 8 9 10 11 12
15 16 17 18 19 20 21	14 15 16 17 18 19 20	13 14 15 16 17 18 19
22 23 24 25 26 27 28	21 22 23 24 25 26 27	20 21 22 23 24 25 26
29 30 31	28 29 30 31	27 28 29 30 31

January 1

January 2

January 3

January 4

January 5

January 6

January 7

Given enough time, what you put off doing today will eventually get done by itself.
— *G. Gestro*

January 8	
January 9	
January 10	
January 11	
January 12	
January 13	
January 14	

January 15	
January 16	
January 17	
January 18	
January 19	
January 20	
January 21	

Today is the tomorrow you worried about yesterday.

Nothing is more vulgar than haste.

—Ralph Waldo Emerson

January 22	
January 23	
January 24	
January 25	
January 26	
January 27	
January 28	

January 29	
January 30	
January 31	

THINGS I FORGOT TO DO THIS MONTH

A Born Procrastinator

Back in 1955, Mrs. Schee of Delaware, Ohio, gave birth to twins — one 48 days after the other.

One for the Books

A belated salute to the fellow who, back in 1823, borrowed a book from the University of Cincinnati Medical Library. With all good intentions, he meant to return it in two weeks. Somehow though, he just never got around to it. Neither did his son. Neither did his grandson.

The family tradition was finally shattered in 1968 when Richard Dodd actually got around to returning the wayward volume.

The overdue fine for 145 years was figured as $2,664 but was waived in honor of establishing a world record.

10 to 1 or 10 'til 1?

A gambler's excuse for being late is a sure bet. There are no clocks in Las Vegas or Atlantic City casinos.

Broken Record

Alan Jay Lerner, the brilliant lyricist of *Camelot* and *Paint Your Wagon,* took two weeks to write the last line of *My Fair Lady's Wouldn't it be Loverly?*. The line he came up with? . . . "loverly, loverly, loverly, loverly."

1989
FEBRUARY
S M T W T F S
1 2 3 4
5 6 7 8 9 10 11
12 13 14 15 16 17 18
19 20 21 22 23 24 25
26 27 28

1990
FEBRUARY
S M T W T F S
1 2 3
4 5 6 7 8 9 10
11 12 13 14 15 16 17
18 19 20 21 22 23 24
25 26 27 28

1991
FEBRUARY
S M T W T F S
1 2
3 4 5 6 7 8 9
10 11 12 13 14 15 16
17 18 19 20 21 22 23
24 25 26 27 28

FEBRUARY

February 1	
February 2	
February 3	
February 4	
February 5	
February 6	
February 7	

Rush is a four letter word.
February 8	
February 9	
February 10	
February 11	
February 12	
February 13	
February 14	

February 15	
February 16	
February 17	
February 18	
February 19	
February 20	
February 21	

Procrastination is the art of keeping up with yesterday. —*Donald Marquis*

Procrastination is the thief of time.
—Edward Young

February 22	
February 23	
February 24	
February 25	
February 26	
February 27	
February 28	

February 29	

THINGS I FORGOT TO DO THIS MONTH

Join The Club

National Procrastination Week, sponsored by the Procrastinators' Club of America, is held annually the first week in March. Les Waas, late president of the club, says, "True procrastinators will celebrate this great event in due time - the second week of March."

You too can actively (or inactively) participate in momentous occasions like this by becoming a member of the Procrastinators' Club.

Among its noble doings in recent years, the club successfully protested the War of 1812, went to the Whitechapel Bell Foundry in London to demand that they honor the warranty on the cracked Liberty Bell, and voyaged to Spain to raise money for 3 ships to discover America.

Proving there's always a future in procrastination, the club looks forward to a National Snail Race (last snail wins) and a visit to Chicago to help put out the fire.

Here's the (s)lowdown on how to apply for membership: (1) Jot down a personal procrastination experience (2) Give a reference who would attest to your procrastination credibility (3) If you have any great ideas for the club, make note of them. Send this information plus $16.00 for membership (due to the inflationary Sixties, the fee just went up a dollar) to: Procrastinators' Club of America, 1111 Broad-Locust Building, Philadelphia, PA 19102.

Sooner or later, you'll receive a membership card, an official License to Procrastinate, and a copy of the club's official publication, *Last Month's Newsletter*.

But Waas warns, "Whatever you do, don't ask us to *rush* your membership card or you'll automatically be disqualified."

1989
MARCH
S M T W T F S
    1 2 3 4
5 6 7 8 9 10 11
12 13 14 15 16 17 18
19 20 21 22 23 24 25
26 27 28 29 30 31

1990
MARCH
S M T W T F S
    1 2 3
4 5 6 7 8 9 10
11 12 13 14 15 16 17
18 19 20 21 22 23 24
25 26 27 28 29 30 31

1991
MARCH
S M T W T F S
    1 2
3 4 5 6 7 8 9
10 11 12 13 14 15 16
17 18 19 20 21 22 23
24 25 26 27 28 29 30
31

MARCH

March
1

March
2

March
3

March
4

March
5

March
6

March
7

You can't get a hen in one morning and have chicken salad for lunch.

—George Humphry

March 8	
March 9	
March 10	
March 11	
March 12	
March 13	
March 14	

March 15	
March 16	
March 17	
March 18	
March 19	
March 20	
March 21	

Haste, haste, has no blessing.

—Swahili Proverb

I've been on a calendar, but never on time.
—Marilyn Monroe

March 22	
March 23	
March 24	
March 25	
March 26	
March 27	
March 28	

March 29	
March 30	
March 31	

THINGS I FORGOT TO DO THIS MONTH

REMINDER –
FILE FOR EXTENSION
APRIL 15

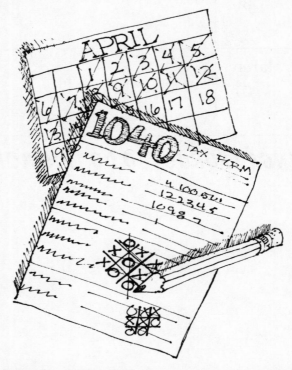

Daylight Savings occurs this month as the time springs forward one hour (perish the thought!). Since you won't be bothering to change your clocks, you'll have time to do this puzzler:

How many times a day do the hands of a clock cross each other?

22. They cross at 12:00, 1:05, 2:11, 3:16, 4:22, 5:27, 6:33, 7:38, 8:44, 9:49, and 10:55 (a.m. & p.m.).

1989
APRIL

S	M	T	W	T	F	S
						1
2	3	4	5	6	7	8
9	10	11	12	13	14	15
16	17	18	19	20	21	22
23	24	25	26	27	28	29
30						

1990
APRIL

S	M	T	W	T	F	S
1	2	3	4	5	6	7
8	9	10	11	12	13	14
15	16	17	18	19	20	21
22	23	24	25	26	27	28
29	30					

1991
APRIL

S	M	T	W	T	F	S
	1	2	3	4	5	6
7	8	9	10	11	12	13
14	15	16	17	18	19	20
21	22	23	24	25	26	27
28	29	30				

APRIL

April
1

April
2

April
3

April
4

April
5

April
6

April
7

Fools rush in where wise men fear to tread.

April 8	
April 9	
April 10	
April 11	
April 12	
April 13	
April 14	

April 15	
April 16	
April 17	
April 18	
April 19	
April 20	
April 21	
Better late than never.	

Forget Domani. Tomorrow never comes.

—F. Sinatra

April 22	
April 23	
April 24	
April 25	
April 26	
April 27	
April 28	

April 29	
April 30	

THINGS I FORGOT TO DO THIS MONTH

Stop the World I Want to Get Off

Procrastinators take heart! Even though others accuse you of moving slowly, you are, in actuality, zipping through space at about 66,700 miles per hour as the Earth orbits the Sun. You are also spinning at about a thousand miles an hour as the Earth rotates. And as if that isn't enough to impress your detractors, you are whirling around the center of the galaxy at roughly eighteen miles a *second!* No wonder you're tired.

Best Two Out of Three?

In 1927, Lawrence Grant and Dr. Munro MacLennan sat down to a chess match at Glasgow University. Since they only get around to making one move apiece per year, the game still hasn't ended.

Low Key Locusts

Learn well the lesson of the cicadas. For seventeen years, these inoffensive little bugs stay nestled underground just sort of hanging out enjoying the quiet life. Then, driven by some instinct from before the dawn of time, they suddenly emerge from the netherworld in a flurry of activity which, naturally, kills them within a couple of weeks.

Procrastinating Pigeon

William S. Wellman of Cleveland, Ohio, entered his new homing pigeon in a hundred mile race in 1939. The bird didn't do so well. In fact, it finished last. In fact, it didn't return home until 1948.

1989
MAY

S	M	T	W	T	F	S
	1	2	3	4	5	6
7	8	9	10	11	12	13
14	15	16	17	18	19	20
21	22	23	24	25	26	27
28	29	30	31			

1990
MAY

S	M	T	W	T	F	S
		1	2	3	4	5
6	7	8	9	10	11	12
13	14	15	16	17	18	19
20	21	22	23	24	25	26
27	28	29	30	31		

1991
MAY

S	M	T	W	T	F	S
			1	2	3	4
5	6	7	8	9	10	11
12	13	14	15	16	17	18
19	20	21	22	23	24	25
26	27	28	29	30	31	

MAY

May
1

May
2

May
3

May
4

May
5

May
6

May
7

Mañana is good enough for me.

—Peggy Lee

May 8	
May 9	
May 10	
May 11	
May 12	
May 13	
May 14	

May 15	
May 16	
May 17	
May 18	
May 19	
May 20	
May 21	

Look before you leap.

Bukra fil mishmish - Arabic for "Leave it for the soft spring when the apricots are blooming."

May 22	
May 23	
May 24	
May 25	
May 26	
May 27	
May 28	

May 29	
May 30	
May 31	

THINGS I FORGOT TO DO THIS MONTH

Procrastinator Quiz

Are you a true PROcrastinator? Take this simple quiz to find out:

1. **When faced with making an important decision do you:**
   a. Take the bull by the horns?   b. Flip a coin?
   c. Hide under your desk until the cleaning lady throws you out?

2. **When do you usually take down your Christmas decorations?**
   a. December 26th.   b. Sometime in January.
   c. The fourth of July (at which time you figure what the heck — it'll be Christmas again in a few months and just leave them up).

3. **When do you usually prepare your tax returns?**
   a. Everything's ready to go by early January.
   b. About 11 P.M. April 14th.
   c. While serving time in a federal pen for failure to file income tax returns.

4. **What statement most closely represents your credo?**
   a. "He who hesitates is lost."   b. "Haste makes waste."
   c. "I'll have to get back to you on that."

5. **When do you figure to start planning for your retirement?**
   a. No time like the present.   b. When you reach 65.
   c. Posthumously.

6. **The intensity of the TV shows you watch can reveal a lot about your metabolic rate. Select your favorite program from the following list:**
   a. *Wide World of Sports.*   b. *Mr. Rogers Neighborhood.*
   c. Test Pattern.

Rating: What's your P.Q.? (Procrastination Quotient)
"A" answers score 1 point.
"B" answers score five points.
"C" answers score twenty points.
Score: 6-20 points - poor procrastinator.
21-45 points - potential procrastinator.
46-120 points - practicing procrastinator.
0 points - A true PROcrastinator - you never got around to taking the quiz!!!

1989
JUNE
S M T W T F S
1 2 3
4 5 6 7 8 9 10
11 12 13 14 15 16 17
18 19 20 21 22 23 24
25 26 27 28 29 30

1990
JUNE
S M T W T F S
1 2
3 4 5 6 7 8 9
10 11 12 13 14 15 16
17 18 19 20 21 22 23
24 25 26 27 28 29 30

1991
JUNE
S M T W T F S
1
2 3 4 5 6 7 8
9 10 11 12 13 14 15
16 17 18 19 20 21 22
23 24 25 26 27 28 29
30

JUNE

June
1

TICKETS

June
2

June
3

June
4

June
5

June
6

June
7

Time is not meant to be devoured in an hour or a day, but to be consumed delicately and gradually and without haste.

—T.H. White

June 8	
June 9	
June 10	
June 11	
June 12	
June 13	
June 14	

June 15	
June 16	
June 17	
June 18	
June 19	
June 20	
June 21	

Procrastination is the habit of resting before fatigue sets in.
—*Jules Renard*

A procrastinator is never bothered by the little things that plague the rest of us - he always waits until they grow into big things.

June 22	
June 23	
June 24	
June 25	
June 26	
June 27	
June 28	

June 29	
June 30	

THINGS I FORGOT TO DO THIS MONTH

Great American Put-Offs

The Federal Government is the state-of-the-art in procrastination. Some cases in point:

Southern General Robert E. Lee was not eligible for amnesty granted to the vanquished combatants of the Civil War, but he did want to rejoin the Union. In order for President Andrew Johnson to grant a pardon, Lee had to send him the oath of allegiance to the Constitution. The General dutifully did so and his citizenship was returned - in 1975, by a special act of Congress, 110 years after the Civil War ended. When Lee died in 1870, he was still a man without a country waiting for an answer.

In related news, Congress, in a generous mood, declared widows of Confederate soldiers eligible to collect veterans pensions (valued in 1983 dollars) of about $70 per month. These pensions were awarded in 1958, 93 years after the war ended.

Uncle Sam danced to an extremely late tune with the *Star Spangled Banner*. Francis Scott Key penned the lyrics in 1813 but it wasn't until 1931 that it was declared the national anthem of the U.S.

In Washington, D.C., they do everything in a big way - including doing nothing.

The cornerstone of the Washington Monument was laid Independence Day, 1848. The building was less than a third completed when privately donated funds ran out in 1856. In 1877, Congress finally got around to appropriating more money and it took another eight years to complete the work. Thus, after 37 years of dilly-dallying, the obelisk was completed in 1885. Also, notice the slight difference in color between the "old" construction and the "new." That's because the long delay forced the stone to be supplied by different quarries.

All in all, a monumental job of putting-off.

1989
JULY
S M T W T F S
                1
2 3 4 5 6 7 8
9 10 11 12 13 14 15
16 17 18 19 20 21 22
23 24 25 26 27 28 29
30 31

1990
JULY
S M T W T F S
1 2 3 4 5 6 7
8 9 10 11 12 13 14
15 16 17 18 19 20 21
22 23 24 25 26 27 28
29 30 31

1991
JULY
S M T W T F S
1 2 3 4 5 6
7 8 9 10 11 12 13
14 15 16 17 18 19 20
21 22 23 24 25 26 27
28 29 30 31

JULY

July
1

July
2

July
3

July
4

July
5

July
6

July
7

Desire to have things done quickly prevents their being done thoroughly.

—*Confucius*

July 8	
July 9	
July 10	
July 11	
July 12	
July 13	
July 14	

July 15	
July 16	
July 17	
July 18	
July 19	
July 20	
July 21	

Some things have to be put off time and time again before they completely slip your mind.

Too swift arrives as tardy as too slow.
—W. Shakespeare

July 22	
July 23	
July 24	
July 25	
July 26	
July 27	
July 28	

July 29	
July 30	
July 31	

THINGS I FORGOT TO DO THIS MONTH

Out of Commission

The genius of geniuses, Leonardo da Vinci, was well known for abandoning work in progress when his commissions ran out. He almost never finished. Fortunately, he didn't get all the money up front from the *Mona Lisa.*

Doubting Thomas

Back in Revolutionary times, Thomas Jefferson wrote a letter to George Washington containing the first American reference to the procrastinator's manifesto - "Delay is preferable to error . . ."

The Naked Truth

Most writers are procrastinators. Even the great wordsmiths find it difficult, and even frightening, to face their most intimidating arch-nemesis, The Blank Page.

Victor Hugo was no exception. He found that he often took a long walk to "clear his mind." He lost so much writing time to his little perambulations, he had to take, pardon the expression, a novel approach.

His servant was given instructions to hide his clothes. And so it was that Victor Hugo became one of the most prolific writers of all the ages, writing his masterworks in the nude.

Seems he might have zipped quicker,
had his desk chair been wicker.

1989
AUGUST
S M T W T F S
1 2 3 4 5
6 7 8 9 10 11 12
13 14 15 16 17 18 19
20 21 22 23 24 25 26
27 28 29 30 31

1990
AUGUST
S M T W T F S
1 2 3 4
5 6 7 8 9 10 11
12 13 14 15 16 17 18
19 20 21 22 23 24 25
26 27 28 29 30 31

1991
AUGUST
S M T W T F S
1 2 3
4 5 6 7 8 9 10
11 12 13 14 15 16 17
18 19 20 21 22 23 24
25 26 27 28 29 30 31

AUGUST

August
1

August
2

August
3

August
4

August
5

August
6

August
7

If you're there before it's over, you're on time.

—James J. Walker

August 8	
August 9	
August 10	
August 11	
August 12	
August 13	
August 14	

August 15	
August 16	
August 17	
August 18	
August 19	
August 20	
August 21	

Hurry can be the assassin of elegance.
—Michael Demarest

What on earth would man do with himself if something did not stand in his way?

—*H.G. Wells*

August 22	
August 23	
August 24	
August 25	
August 26	
August 27	
August 28	

August 29	
August 30	
August 31	

THINGS I FORGOT TO DO THIS MONTH

Work Work Work

Work is the greatest thing in the world, so we should always save some of it for tomorrow.

—Don Herold

Hard work never killed anybody, but why take a chance?

—Charlie McCarthy (Edgar Bergen)

I like work; it fascinates me. I can sit and look at it for hours.

—Jerome K. Jerome

One of the greatest labor-saving inventions of today is tomorrow.

—Vincent T. Foss

Work is the refuge of people who have nothing better to do.

—Oscar Wilde

All work and no play makes Jack a dull boy.

—James Howell

Anyone can do any amount of work provided it isn't the work he is supposed to be doing at that moment.

—Robert Benchley

The world is full of willing people; some willing to work, the rest willing to let them.

—Robert Frost

The trouble with unemployment is that the minute you wake up in the morning you're on the job.

—Slappy White

1989
SEPTEMBER
S M T W T F S
| | | | | | 1 2
3 4 5 6 7 8 9
10 11 12 13 14 15 16
17 18 19 20 21 22 23
24 25 26 27 28 29 30

1990
SEPTEMBER
S M T W T F S
| | | | | | 1
2 3 4 5 6 7 8
9 10 11 12 13 14 15
16 17 18 19 20 21 22
23 24 25 26 27 28 29
30

1991
SEPTEMBER
S M T W T F S
1 2 3 4 5 6 7
8 9 10 11 12 13 14
15 16 17 18 19 20 21
22 23 24 25 26 27 28
29 30

SEPTEMBER

September
1

September
2

September
3

September
4

September
5

September
6

September
7

An artist's career always begins tomorrow.

—James Whistler

September 8	
September 9	
September 10	
September 11	
September 12	
September 13	
September 14	

September 15	
September 16	
September 17	
September 18	
September 19	
September 20	
September 21	

Never put off till tomorrow what you can do the day after tomorrow. —*Mark Twain*

Start slow and taper off.

—*Walt Stack*

September 22	
September 23	
September 24	
September 25	
September 26	
September 27	
September 28	

September 29	
September 30	

THINGS I FORGOT TO DO THIS MONTH

Killing Time

The clock shown here was smashed to smithereens, unquestionably by someone who had absolutely no regard for time. See if you can pick up the pieces and figure out what time it was when the clock was struck.

While you're at it, you might as well be reminded that you get to move the clock back one hour the last Sunday of this month. Hallelujah! One more hour to put off until tomorrow things you should have done today.

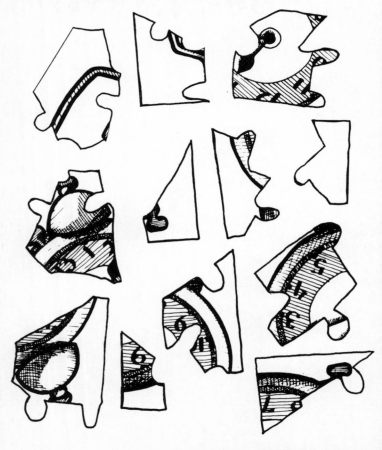

The clock was struck at 13:10 (and we don't mean military time). When procrastinators say "add an hour," they really mean it!

1989
OCTOBER
S M T W T F S
1 2 3 4 5 6 7
8 9 10 11 12 13 14
15 16 17 18 19 20 21
22 23 24 25 26 27 28
29 30 31

1990
OCTOBER
S M T W T F S
1 2 3 4 5 6
7 8 9 10 11 12 13
14 15 16 17 18 19 20
21 22 23 24 25 26 27
28 29 30 31

1991
OCTOBER
S M T W T F S
1 2 3 4 5
6 7 8 9 10 11 12
13 14 15 16 17 18 19
20 21 22 23 24 25 26
27 28 29 30 31

OCTOBER

October
1

October
2

October
3

October
4

October
5

October
6

October
7

Never do today what you can do tomorrow. Something may occur to make you regret your premature action. —*Aaron Burr*

October 8	
October 9	
October 10	
October 11	
October 12	
October 13	
October 14	

October 15	
October 16	
October 17	
October 18	
October 19	
October 20	
October 21	

Never keep up with the Joneses. Drag them down to your level.   —*Quentin Crisp*

Procrastination is a fault that most people put off trying to correct.

—Indianapolis *News*

October 22	
October 23	
October 24	
October 25	
October 26	
October 27	
October 28	

October 29	
October 30	
October 31	

THINGS I FORGOT TO DO THIS MONTH

General Postponement

A Roman general by the name of Quintus Fabius Maximus was famous for putting off battle until the last possible moment. For this, his troops dubbed him "Cunctator" (Delayer).

Teeny Bopper Stopper

A belated salute to J.V. Walker, a public health officer in England who proposed a pubescent postponement pill to delay puberty until the completion of college. Seems the theory is that studies would go better without all those hormones mucking up one's brain.

In a way the proposition worked. It did manage to put off most people.

By Gosh, We Love Oshkosh!

There's always a warm welcome for procrastinators in Oshkosh, Nebraska. The town has adopted the motto "Where there is always nothing doing."

Motheaten Mozart

The music world has always marched to the beat of its own drummer. It deserves special recognition for putting off the proper performance of Mozart's *"Organ Piece for a Clock."*

Composition was completed March 3, 1791, and it wasn't performed as intended until October 9, 1982. Now we know why there are so many symphonies that composers just never bothered to finish.

And the beat goes on and on and on . . .

Johannes Brahms dawdled over composing his first symphony for almost twenty years.

1989
NOVEMBER
S M T W T F S
          1 2 3 4
5 6 7 8 9 10 11
12 13 14 15 16 17 18
19 20 21 22 23 24 25
26 27 28 29 30

1990
NOVEMBER
S M T W T F S
             1 2 3
4 5 6 7 8 9 10
11 12 13 14 15 16 17
18 19 20 21 22 23 24
25 26 27 28 29 30

1991
NOVEMBER
S M T W T F S
                1 2
3 4 5 6 7 8 9
10 11 12 13 14 15 16
17 18 19 20 21 22 23
24 25 26 27 28 29 30

NOVEMBER

November
1

November
2

November
3

November
4

November
5

November
6

November
7

If it weren't for the last minute, nothing would get done.

November 8	
November 9	
November 10	
November 11	
November 12	
November 13	
November 14	

November 15	
November 16	
November 17	
November 18	
November 19	
November 20	
November 21	

Punctuality is the thief of time. —*Oscar Wilde*

It is impossible to enjoy idling unless there is plenty of work to do. —*Jerome K. Jerome*

November 22	
November 23	
November 24	
November 25	
November 26	
November 27	
November 28	

November 29	
November 30	

THINGS I FORGOT TO DO THIS MONTH

Last Laughs

Book salesman: "This book will do half your work for you!"
Procrastinator: "Good, I'll take two!"

A procrastinator's idea of Happy Hour is a nap.

The only thing a procrastinator exercises is caution.

A procrastinator's memory is what makes them wonder what it is they've forgotten to put off.

Procrastination is my sin.
It brings me endless sorrow
I really must stop doing it -
in fact I'll start tomorrow!

If someone never put things off, would they be called an anti-crastinator?

Boss: "Johnson - look at you - sitting at your desk just staring into space - you're procrastinating, always procrastinating!
Johnson: "Hey, it beats doing nothing!"

Q: What's the difference between a bureaucrat and a chess player?
A: A chess player moves once in a while.

There were procrastinators even in Revolutionary War days. In fact, they had their own unit. You've probably heard of them - The Last Minutemen.

You've heard, of course, about the young woman who procrastinated in EVERYTHING. She's the mother of triplets aged seven, eight and nine.

Watson's Law: A committee is a group acting collectively to delay a conclusion.

Then there was the case of the procrastinating proctologist who got behind in his work.

Have you heard about the new support group called Procrastinator's Anonymous? Whenever you feel like you're about to put something off, you call another member and in a couple of weeks they come over to talk.

1989
DECEMBER
S M T W T F S
          1 2
3 4 5 6 7 8 9
10 11 12 13 14 15 16
17 18 19 20 21 22 23
24 25 26 27 28 29 30
31

1990
DECEMBER
S M T W T F S
             1
2 3 4 5 6 7 8
9 10 11 12 13 14 15
16 17 18 19 20 21 22
23 24 25 26 27 28 29
30 31

1991
DECEMBER
S M T W T F S
1 2 3 4 5 6 7
8 9 10 11 12 13 14
15 16 17 18 19 20 21
22 23 24 25 26 27 28
29 30 31

DECEMBER

December 1	
December 2	
December 3	
December 4	
December 5	
December 6	
December 7	

After all is said and done, more is said than done.

December 8	
December 9	
December 10	
December 11	
December 12	
December 13	
December 14	

December 15	
December 16	
December 17	
December 18	
December 19	
December 20	
December 21	

There is no pleasure in having nothing to do; the fun is having lots to do and not doing it.
—*John W. Raper*

Five minutes after I'm there, they'll forget I was late.

—Marilyn Monroe

December 22	
December 23	
December 24	
December 25	
December 26	
December 27	
December 28	

December 29	
December 30	
December 31	

THINGS I FORGOT TO DO THIS MONTH

All in a Day's Shirk

This is an invaluable aid to the true procrastinator. Use the spaces provided to keep track of those days when you were *not* late for work, class or other important stuff during the year. You might also want to note work finished on time or projects handed in by deadline. Once completed, you can assess your performance at a glance and vow to have a blanker page next year.

January

_____
_____
_____
_____

February

_____
_____
_____
_____

March

_____
_____
_____
_____

April

_____
_____
_____
_____

May

_____
_____
_____
_____

June

_____
_____
_____
_____

July

_____

August

_____

September

_____

October

_____

November

_____

December

_____

Emergency Doodle Page

Procrastinator's Horoscope

Sometimes procrastination is a tricky business. After all, making a decision not to do anything is, in fact, doing something in itself. Then, there's always the messy matter of justification - coming up with excuses not to do something. Well, procrastinator, relax - your troubles are over - this handy dandy perpetual horoscope will provide you with just the rationalization you seek.

Capricorn (The Goat)
Born Dec. 22 - Jan. 19

You are a person of great ambition. Unfortunately, your ruling planet is Saturn where a year is 29 Earth years. Naturally, you seem to move a bit slow to terrestrial observers. Out on the ringed planet though, you'd be a real go-getter. It's very important that you avoid doing anything whatsoever today. What are you still reading for? You're not supposed to do anything more - close your eyes - just stop and rest!

Aquarius (The Water Carrier)
Born Jan. 20 - Feb. 18

In actuality, the dawning of the Age of Aquarius isn't for quite a few years yet so you've got plenty of time to get ready. You are "The Water Carrier" but that doesn't necessarily make you a drip. You are well advised to shun any new venture today, or any old venture for that matter. Minimize activity and don't make any rash judgments -unless you are a dermatologist.

Pisces (The Fish)
Born Feb. 19 - March 20

Your best day for successful completion of projects is February 29th., except in Leap Year when it's February 30th. Attempt nothing on any other day.

Aries (The Ram)
Born March 21 - April 19

You are decisive and aggressive, a mover and shaker, a real Type A personality - used to stress and adversity. Consequently, any action you take today could bring on a fatal heart attack. . .

Taurus (The Bull)
Born April 20 - May 20

Ruled as you are by Venus, a planet with less gravity pull than Earth, you have a tough time sticking to anything. In order to avoid being a real yo-yo, you should be put in your place - and kept there. Productive movement is futile!

Gemini (The Twins)
Born May 21 - June 20

Born under the sign of the twins you are at once shrewd but gullible, industrious but lazy, adventurous but timid. Therefore your entire personality cancels itself out. Go back to sleep.

Cancer (The Crab)
Born June 21 - July 22

Born under this sign you are a Moonchild and as such, you're only bright about once a month. The twentieth century is a bad time for travel, investment, love, career and health. Suggest you investigate cryogenics.

Leo (The Lion)
Born July 23 - Aug. 22
Ruled by the Sun, Leos are subject to spontaneous combustion. Any excessive activity and poof!

Virgo (The Virgin)
Born Aug. 23 - Sept. 22
As your sign implies, you are naturally good at doing nothing. To stay out of trouble, keep it that way.

Libra (The Scales)
Born Sept. 23 - Oct. 22
You've been a procrastinator since you were born. In fact, you should have been a Taurus. The stars say it is a Libra who is destined to inadvertently start World War III. Don't take any chances - stay perfectly still, just slowly lower this book and stare straight ahead. We'll get back to you.

Scorpio (The Scorpion)
Born Oct. 23 - Nov. 21
Some people are meant to shape history, to move mountains and to inspire greatness in their countrymen. Then there are Scorpios. Aptitude tests show them to make excellent couch potatoes. Unquestionably the low point of the Zodiac, Scorpios should never make policy decisions or be allowed near sharp objects.

Sagittarius (The Archer)
Born Nov. 22 - Dec. 21
The essential ingredient of any endeavor is planning. Be it work, school or pleasure, it must be well thought out. Sagittarians are masters of meditation. They may appear to be sleeping but, in reality, they are on a higher plane of consciousness. Let sleeping Sagittarians lie.

Time Zones

Alaska

4 am

Atlantic
10 am

Central

Eastern

Pacific

6 am

Mountain

7 am

8 am

9 am

Amazing Fact

Procrastinators aren't necessarily late - just a couple of time zones out of phase. But before 1883, even the most punctual traveler had a rough go of it being in the right place at the right time. Up 'til then, there were not four time zones in the continental United States, but four *score*. Back then, there was no standard time; high noon occurred whenever the sun crossed the meridian overhead. When it was noon in Boston, it was 11:36 a.m. in Washington, D.C., and a different time in 78 other zones in the U.S.

This time craziness played havoc with railroads and their time schedules. Finally, one Charles F. Dowd published *A System of National Time for Railroads* which was adopted in 1883 and utilized the four time zones as we know them today.

Names and Numbers

Here's a place to list all those important names, addresses and phone numbers that you'll probably never get around to using. In addition, there's space to jot down a good excuse as to why you haven't returned their calls just in case they ever do manage to nail you on the phone.

Sample excuses: Sorry, I didn't get a single one of your 18 messages.

There's a wiretap on my phone so I didn't want to call and get you involved in this thing.

Hey - Hi there! Wow! You're a hard person to reach. I must've tried a dozen times to return your call.

Your call-forwarding must be on the blink. Every time I returned your call, I got the Kremlin.

Name and Address	Telephone Number	Excuse For Not Returning Call

Name and Address	Telephone Number	Excuse For Not Returning Call

Name and Address	Telephone Number	Excuse For Not Returning Call

Name and Address	Telephone Number	Excuse For Not Returning Call

Name and Address	Telephone Number	Excuse For Not Returning Call

Name and Address	Telephone Number	Excuse For Not Returning Call

Name and Address	Telephone Number	Excuse For Not Returning Call

Name and Address	Telephone Number	Excuse For Not Returning Call

Commonly Overlooked Holidays

Holiday	1989	1990	1991
New Year's Day	Sun/Jan 1	Mon/Jan 1	Tues/Jan 1
Martin Luther King, Jr. Day	Mon/Jan 16	Mon/Jan 15	Mon/Jan 21
Ground-Hog Day	Thu/Feb 2	Fri/Feb 2	Sat/Feb 2
Valentine's Day	Tue/Feb 14	Wed/Feb 14	Thu/Feb 14
Presidents Day	Mon/Feb 20	Mon/Feb 19	Mon/Feb 18
St. Patrick's Day	Fri/Mar 17	Sat/Mar 17	Sun/Mar 17
Passover	Thu/Apr 20	Tue/Apr 10	Sat/Mar 30
Easter Sunday	Sun/Mar 26	Sun/Apr 15	Sun/Mar 31
Mother's Day	Sun/May 14	Sun/May 13	Sun/May 12
Victoria Day (Canada)	Mon/May 22	Mon/May 21	Mon/May 20
Memorial Day (Observed)	Mon/May 29	Mon/May 28	Mon/May 27
Flag Day	Wed/Jun 14	Thu/Jun 14	Fri/Jun 14
Father's Day	Sun/Jun 18	Sun/Jun 17	Sun/Jun 16
Canada Day (Canada)	Sat/Jul 1	Sun/Jul 1	Mon/Jul 1
Independence Day	Tue/Jul 4	Wed/Jul 4	Thu/Jul 4
Labor Day	Mon/Sep 4	Mon/Sep 3	Mon/Sep 2
Rosh Hashanah	Sat/Sep 30	Thu/Sep 20	Mon/Sep 9
Yom Kippur	Mon/Oct 9	Sat/Sep 29	Wed/Sep 18
Columbus Day (Observed)	Mon/Oct 9	Mon/Oct 8	Mon/Oct 14
Thanksgiving Day (Canada)	Mon/Oct 9	Mon/Oct 8	Mon/Oct 14
Halloween	Tue/Oct 31	Wed/Oct 31	Thu/Oct 31
Election Day	Tue/Nov 7	Tue/Nov 6	Tue/Nov 5
Veterans Day	Sat/Nov 11	Sun/Nov 11	Mon/Nov 11
Thanksgiving Day	Thu/Nov 23	Thu/Nov 22	Thu/Nov 28
Hanukkah	Sat/Dec 23	Wed/Dec 12	Mon/Dec 2
Christmas Day	Mon/Dec 25	Tue/Dec 25	Wed/Dec 25

Read All About
Earthly Oddities

THE OZONE LAYER

Patricia Armentrout

The Rourke Press, Inc.
Vero Beach, Florida 32964

PHOTO CREDITS
© Armentrout: pgs. 10, 19, 21; © CASE International: pg. 18; © East Coast Studios: pg. 12; © Andre Jenny/Int'l Stock: pg. 15; © Chuck Mason/Int'l Stock: pg. 4; © NASA: Cover, pg. 9; © James P. Rowan: pg. 13; © Valder/Tormey/Int'l Stock: pg. 16; © Oscar C. Williams: pgs. 6, 7, 22

ACKNOWLEDGMENTS
The author wishes to acknowledge David Armentrout for his contribution in writing this book.

Library of Congress Cataloging-in-Publication Data

Armentrout, Patricia, 1960-
     The ozone layer / by Patricia Armentrout.
       p. cm. — (Earthly Oddities)
     Includes index.
     Summary: Describes the ozone layer, explains how it is broken down, and suggests ways to reduce air pollution.
       ISBN 1-57103-156-1
     1. Ozone layer—Juvenile literature. 2. Air—Pollution—Juvenile literature. [1. Ozone layer. 2. Air—Pollution. 3. Pollution.]
I. Title II. Series: Armentrout, Patricia, 1960- Earthly Oddities.
QC881.2.09A73 1996
363.73'92—dc20   96–2883
                                                                      CIP
                                                                       AC

Printed in the USA

TABLE OF CONTENTS

OZONE GAS

Ozone is a form of **oxygen** (AHK suh jen). It is a gas. Ozone is formed in the lower **atmosphere** (AT muh SFEER) when sunlight mixes with other gases and chemicals. Atmosphere is another word for air.

Too much ozone gas is dangerous to people when it is at ground level. Ozone gas at ground level is air pollution. Ozone gas is in dirty, smelly air called smog.

Ozone gas is formed when sunlight mixes with gases and chemicals from car exhausts.

THE OZONE LAYER

The Earth has its own natural blanket of protection called the ozone layer. The ozone layer is about 20 miles above the Earth's surface. The ozone layer is made up of high levels of ozone gas.

The ozone layer protects people from the sun's harmful rays.

Plants could not survive without the Earth's protective ozone layer.

The ozone in the Earth's upper atmosphere helps people on Earth, instead of being a danger to them. The ozone layer absorbs some of the sun's harmful rays before they reach Earth. Without this protection from the sun's rays, Earth would be an impossible place to live for people and plants.

A HOLE IN THE OZONE LAYER

Man-made gases and chemicals are released into the air. Experts say that when such gases rise into the upper atmosphere they destroy the Earth's protective ozone shield.

In the 1970's, after many studies of chemicals and gases, scientists warned people of a possible breakdown of the ozone layer. Then in the mid 1980's a hole in the ozone layer was discovered above **Antarctica** (ant AHRK ti kuh). By 1988, experts said the ozone layer was thinning around the entire globe.

The purple color on this ozone chart shows the thinning areas of the Earth's ozone layer.

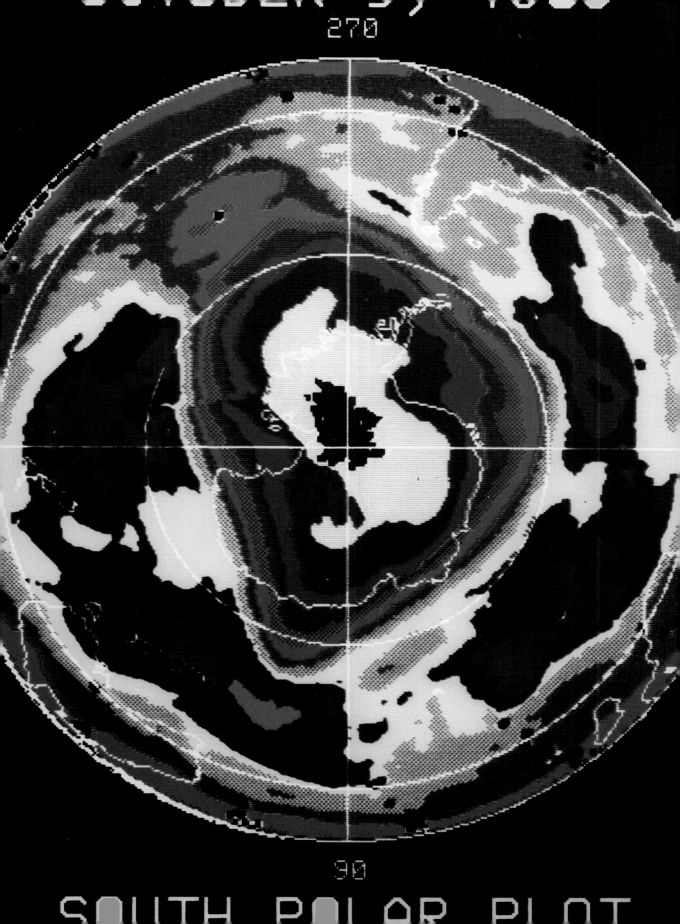

90

SOUTH POLAR PLOT

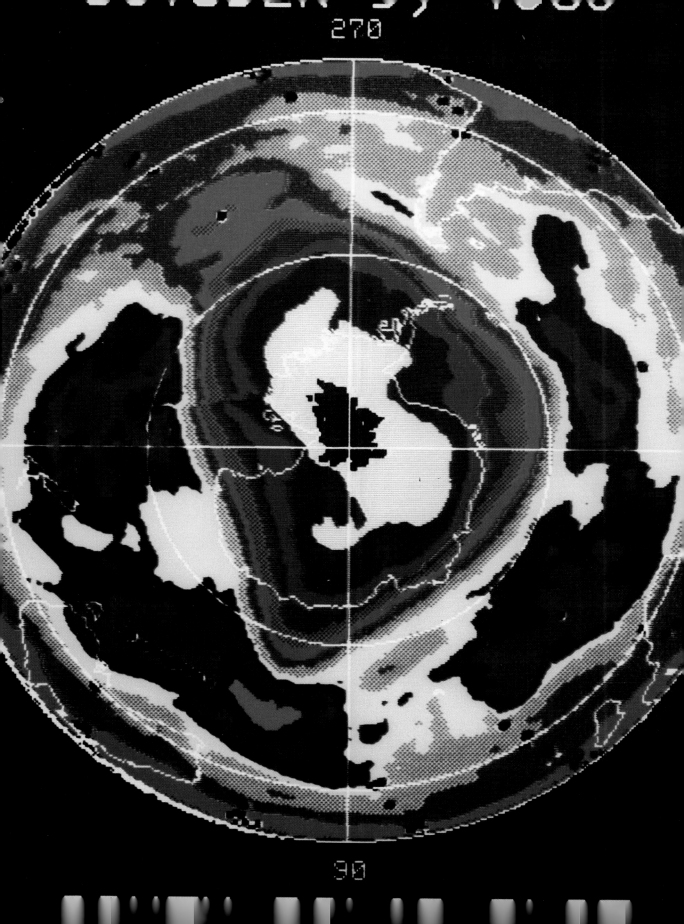

AEROSOLS

What do whipped cream and deodorant have in common? Sometimes they come in **aerosol** (AIR uh sawl) containers. Aerosols are products forced out of their containers by a gas, called a **propellant** (pruh PEL unt). Chlorine, fluorine, and carbon chemicals mix to make a propellant known as CFC's.

Imagine yourself fixing an ice cream sundae. You reach for the can of whipped cream and press down on the nozzle. With each press of the nozzle, whipped cream comes out, as well as the invisible gas. The CFC's rise to the upper atmosphere. Scientists say CFC's are causing the ozone layer to break down.

The pump spray bottles on the right do not use propellants that release harmful chemicals.

SMOG

Smog is a kind of pollution in our air. It is a blend of smoke and fog. Smog is common in cities with a lot of factories and many cars.

Cutting grass in the bright hours of the day increases the formation of ozone gas.

Boats with gas-powered engines contribute to ozone and air pollution.

Cars, trucks, boats, and gas-powered lawn mowers release several gases from their exhaust pipes. Two of the gases are called **nitrogen oxide** (NY truh jen) (AHK syd) and **hydrocarbons** (HY druh KAHR bunz). When these gases mix with light from the sun, they produce ozone gas. Ozone combines with other pollutants to form smog.

ACID RAIN

What happens when a smoggy day gets rained out? The air seems fresher, as though all the pollution has been washed away. But pollution never really goes away. Chemicals are always in the air. They settle on plants and food crops and get into our lakes and rivers.

Mother nature starts her cycle again. Moisture is evaporated into the air, taking harmful chemicals with it. It comes down again as acid rain. Acid rain is polluted rain that pours harmful chemicals on the Earth's surface.

The chemicals in acid rain harm plants and crops and even destroy forests.

OZONE, POLLUTION, AND PEOPLE

We know that ozone is a gas that helps protect the Earth when it is miles above the surface. But when it is in the air we breathe, ozone is pollution. The lower level ozone does not rise to become the upper ozone layer.

High ozone levels and polluted air can sting the eyes and make breathing difficult. Some cities have days when weather forecasters warn people to stay inside. Pollution can be seen in the air, especially on hot summer days.

Some factories have contributed to air pollution.

CLEANER AIR

Now that we know the ozone layer is being destroyed, scientists and industry are working together to help keep our air cleaner. One example is farming. Some farmers now grow corn to produce **ethanol** (ETH uh NAWL). Ethanol is a clear liquid that is mixed with gasoline. Ethanol burns cleaner than gas, which means fewer harmful chemicals coming out of car exhausts.

Corn is harvested and used in the production of ethanol.

Gasoline mixed with ethanol is a cleaner burning fuel.

Other industries are helping too. Companies that make aerosols no longer use harmful CFC's. Some countries have outlawed the use of CFC's altogether.

WHAT CAN WE DO?

Everyone can do his or her part to reduce air pollution.

Walking, riding a bike, carpooling, or taking a bus will cut down on exhaust in our air. Less car exhaust means less ozone in the lower atmosphere.

Use pump sprays instead of aerosols. Pump containers don't contain CFC's that harm our upper ozone shield.

Save energy whenever possible. Using less electricity means that power plants burn less fuel, and fewer chemicals and gases will escape into our air.

Using an electric lawn mower is one way to reduce the amount of ozone gas in our air.

GLOSSARY

Antarctica (ant AHRK ti kuh) — the fifth largest continent located at the South Pole, which has the world's coldest climate

atmosphere (AT muh SFEER) — the air surrounding Earth

aerosol (AIR uh sawl) — a product that comes out of its container by gas pressure

ethanol (ETH uh NAWL) — a liquid fuel made from corn that is mixed with gasoline

hydrocarbons (HY druh KAHR bunz) — a mix of chemicals and a colorless, odorless gas called hydrogen

nitrogen oxide (NY truh jen) (AHK syd) — a tasteless, odorless gas containing oxygen

oxygen (AHK suh jen) — a colorless, odorless gas that is essential for life

propellant (pruh PEL unt) — a gas used in aerosol cans that pushes or forces the contents out

The Earth's ozone layer protects people and plants from the sun's harmful rays.

23

INDEX